Uniquely Louisiana

Donna Loughran

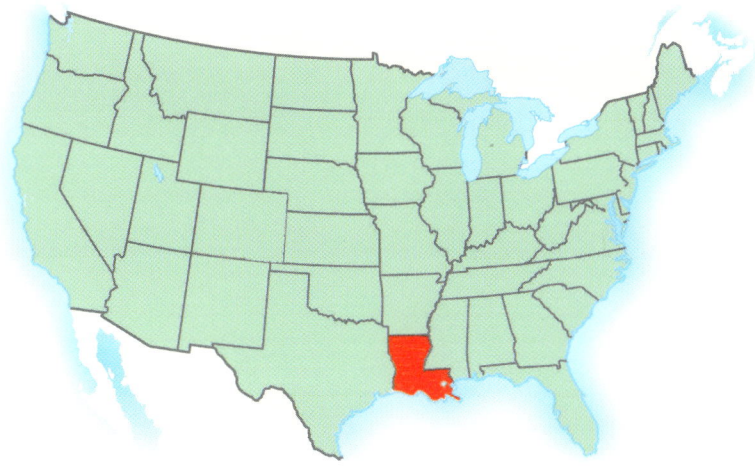

Heinemann Library
Chicago, Illinois

© 2004 Heinemann Library
a division of Reed Elsevier Inc.
Chicago, Illinois

Customer Service 888-454-2279

Visit our website at www.heinemannlibrary.com

All rights reserved. No part of this publication may be reproduced or transmitted in any form or by any means, electronic or mechanical, including photocopying, recording, taping, or any information storage and retrieval system, without permission in writing from the publisher.

Designed by Heinemann Library
Printed and bound in the United States by Lake Book Manufacturing, Inc.

08 07 06 05 04
10 9 8 7 6 5 4 3 2 1

Library of Congress Cataloging-in-Publication Data

Loughran, Donna.
   Uniquely Louisiana / Donna Loughran.
      p. cm.—(Heinemann state studies)
Summary: Provides an overview of various aspects of Louisiana that make it a unique state, including its people, land, government, culture, economy, and attractions.
Includes bibliographical references and index.
   ISBN 1-4034-4492-7 (HC library binding)—
ISBN 1-4034-4507-9 (PB)
   1. Louisiana—Juvenile literature. [1. Louisiana.]
I. Title. II. Series.
   F369.3.L67 2003
   976.3--dc21
                                         2003009431

Cover Pictures

Top (left to right) *Magnolia, Louisiana fisher, Louisiana state flag, Mardi Gras parade in New Orleans* **Main** *Oak Alley Plantation in Vacherie*

Acknowledgments
Development and photo research by
BOOK BUILDERS LLC

The author and publishers are grateful to the following for permission to reproduce copyrighted material:

Cover photographs by (top, L-R) Courtesy Louisiana Office of Tourism; Philip Gould/Corbis; Courtesy Louisiana Office of Tourism; Courtesy Louisiana Office of Tourism; (main) Courtesy Louisiana Office of Tourism.

Title page (L-R); Courtesy Louisiana Office of Tourism; Goodshoot/Alamy Images; Philip Gould/Corbis; contents page Courtesy Louisiana Office of Tourism; p. 4 Alex S. MacLean/Peter Arnold Inc.; pp. 5, 6, 8, 15, 44 Alex Demyan; pp. 7B, 13T, 22 C. C. Lockwood; pp. 7T, 41, 45 IMA for Book Builders LLC; pp. 9, 10, 11, 12T, 12M, 12B, 14T, 16, 20, 21B, 39 Courtesy Louisiana Office of Tourism; p. 13B Ehlers/Photo Network; p. 14B David Wasserman/Alamy Images; pp. 17, 18, 19B, 32 Bettmann/Corbis; pp. 19T, 27, 30, 38 Philip Gould/Corbis; pp. 21T, 34 Andre Jenny/Alamy Images; p. 24 Courtesy the Louisiana Supreme Court; p. 25 Popperfoto/Alamy Images; p. 26 Fred Maroon/Photo Researchers; p. 28 Blair Seitz/Photo Researchers; p. 31 The Image Bank/Getty Images; p. 33 William Holbrook Beard, *Nights With Uncle Remus*, 1911; p. 35 Gregory Shamus/NBAE/Getty Images; p. 36 Steve Franz/LSU Sports Information; p. 37 Getty Images; p. 40 Courtesy Shelby Gilley; p. 42 Goodshoot/Alamy Images; p. 43 Joy Tessman

Special thanks to Florent Hardy, Louisiana State Archivist and Director, for her expert comments in the preparation of this book.

Every effort has been made to contact copyright holders of any material reproduced in this book. Any omissions will be rectified in subsequent printings if notice is given to the publisher.

Some words are shown in bold, **like this.** You can find out what they mean by looking in the glossary.

Contents

Uniquely Louisiana 4
Louisiana's Geography and Climate 6
Famous Firsts 8
Louisiana's State Symbols 10
Louisiana's History and People 15
The French Quarter 20
Louisiana's State Government 22
Louisiana's Culture 25
Louisiana's Food 29
Louisiana's Folklore and Legends 32
Louisiana's Sports Teams 34
Louisiana's Businesses and Products 37
Attractions and Landmarks 40
Map of Louisiana 45
Glossary 46
More Books to Read 47
Index 48
About the Authors . . 48

Uniquely Louisiana

Visitors to Louisiana often feel as if they have entered a different country. Airport announcements are in French and English. At the food court, the menu includes strange-sounding foods such as *étouffée, gumbo,* and *boudin.* The differences reveal why Louisiana is unique—a one-of-a-kind state.

ORIGIN OF THE STATE'S NAME

Louisiana's past is reflected in its name. In 1682 René-Robert Cavelier, **Sieur de LaSalle,** traveled down the Mississippi River from Canada. After reaching the Gulf of Mexico, he claimed the river and the land around it for King Louis XIV of France. LaSalle called the land *Louisiana* in honor of his king.

MAJOR CITIES

Louisiana's three largest cities are home to about half of the state's population. Baton Rouge is the capital of Louisiana and its second largest city. French explorer Pierre Le Moyne, **Sieur de Iberville,** gave the city its

Oil from Oklahoma, Texas, and Louisiana is processed in Baton Rouge. After the discovery of oil in Louisiana in 1902, oil refineries sprang up in the city.

name in 1699. After coming upon a post smeared with animal blood, Iberville learned that it marked the border between two Native American tribes. He called the city that grew up there "Baton Rouge," "red stick" in French. Today Baton Rouge is a major port.

With a population of nearly 500,000, New Orleans is Louisiana's largest city. It is located on the Gulf of Mexico at the mouth of the Mississippi–Missouri river system. People use the rivers to ship goods to other countries. Those goods enter and leave the nation through New Orleans, the second leading commercial port in the Americas. The city is unique in yet another way. At 8 feet below sea level, it is the second lowest point in the United States. Huge **levees** 25 feet high protect the city from floods. Without them, New Orleans would not exist.

Shreveport was founded in 1837. The city is named for Henry Shreve, a riverboat captain who opened the city to steamboat traffic by clearing a 165-mile jam of dirt and wood from the river. Today, **oil refining** is Shreveport's largest industry. The city is also a research center. Intertech, a planned 2,400-acre international research park, contains three large medical centers and other research facilities.

Shreveport is located on the Red River in northwestern Louisiana.

Louisiana's Geography and Climate

Louisiana's shape is constantly changing. The Mississippi River carries 400 million cubic yards of mud, sand, and gravel each year to the Gulf of Mexico, building land along its path. At the same time, gulf waters nibble away at the state's southern coastline.

LAND

The Mississippi **Delta** stretches from Arkansas in the north to the Gulf of Mexico in the south. Louisiana's two other main regions are the Eastern Coastal Plain and the Western Coastal Plain. The Eastern Coastal Plain includes the land east of the Mississippi River and north of salty Lake Pontchartrain.

The Western Coastal Plain is Louisiana's largest region and has hills covered with oak, elm, and pine trees.

Lake Pontchartrain covers 625 square miles. It is about the size of 200 football fields.

Average Annual Precipitation Louisiana

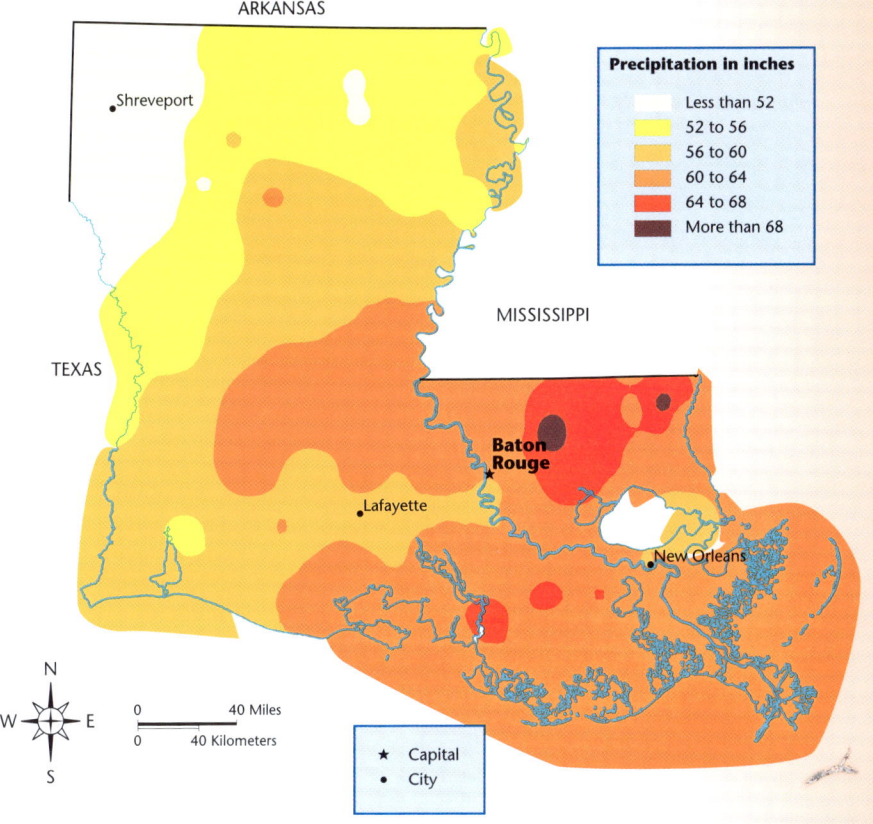

The average precipitation in the United States is about 29 inches per year. Louisiana is one of the wettest states in the nation.

CLIMATE

The Gulf of Mexico, which forms Louisiana's southern border, influences the state's climate. In July Louisiana's average temperature is around 82°F. The air is thick with moisture from the Gulf of Mexico. Together, the heat and moisture make the summer air feel like a wet blanket. In winter temperatures are mild, around 50°F (10°C).

The Sleeping Waters of Louisiana

The Choctaw, a Native American tribe, called the slow-moving streams found across Louisiana *bayuk*. French settlers changed the word to *bayou*. A bayou is a wetland with trees, shrubs, or grass growing around or in it. A bayou is connected to a larger body of water, such as a river, lake, or sea. About 45 percent of the nation's **wetlands** are in Louisiana.

Famous Firsts

In 1796 North America's first grand opera performance took place in New Orleans in the old French Opera House. An opera is a play set to music. The Mahalia Jackson Theater of the Performing Arts now stands on the site of the old opera house that burned down in 1919.

English settlers in Louisiana organized the Tally-Ho Club in New Orleans in 1815. It is the oldest hunting and fishing club in the United States. Its name comes from a tradition in English fox hunting. Riders on horseback shout "Tally-Ho" when a fox is sighted.

The Lake Pontchartrain **Causeway** consists of two bridges that run side by side across the lake. Completed in 1956 and 1969, the double causeway spans 24 miles from New Orleans to Mandeville. It is the longest overwater bridge in the world.

The Lake Pontchartrain Causeway is supported by 9,000 concrete pilings, or columns.

The oldest salt mine in the Americas is on Avery Island, just off the coast of Louisiana. Discovered in 1862, Avery is not really an island but a huge dome of rock salt. There are more than 200 salt domes in Louisiana. They began to form millions of years ago when salt dropped from the shallow sea that once covered most of the state.

In 1868 Edmund McIlhenny, a retired New Orleans banker who lived on Avery Island, grew red peppers as a hobby. He used the peppers to make different kinds of sauces. He called one of his fiery hot pepper sauces *Tabasco*. Historians think it may mean "land where the soil is hot and humid" or "place of coral or oyster shell." The first batch of Tabasco sauce numbered only a few hundred bottles. Today more than 60 million bottles are turned out each year.

Over two days, April 6–7, 1893, the longest boxing match in history took place in New Orleans. Jack Burke and Andy Bowen boxed for 7 hours and 19 minutes over 110 rounds. The match ended in a tie.

Louisiana is home to the only known white alligators in the world. In 1987 a fisherman in a bayou in Terrebonne Parish saw a pure white alligator. Although alligators have been around for about 70 million years, this was the first recorded sighting of a white one. Scientists believe that white alligators are rare because their coloring makes them easy for hungry herons and turtles to spot.

Today there are about 500 white alligators in Louisiana's wetlands.

Louisiana's State Symbols

State Motto: "Union, Justice, and Confidence"

In 1902 lawmakers chose "Union, Justice, and Confidence" as the state motto. The word *Union* reflects Louisiana's loyalty to the United States. *Justice* speaks to the state's commitment to protect the rights of all its citizens. The word *Confidence* reveals the state's belief in itself and its bright future.

Louisiana State Seal

A seal is a stamp that shows that a government paper is an official document. William C.C. Claiborne, the first governor of the Louisiana Territory and later the state of Louisiana, was the first to use a seal that showed a pelican family. He chose it because a mother pelican is said to use her own flesh to feed her chicks if food is scarce. In 1803 Claiborne decided that the mother pelican's dedication to her young was a good way to represent Louisiana's concerns for its people's welfare. In 1902 the Louisiana lawmakers approved the current seal.

Over the years, government departments have used different pictures of the pelican on seals. The one shown here is on the state's official seal.

Louisiana has had ten official flags, including the current one.

LOUISIANA STATE FLAG

Louisiana's current flag became the official flag in 1912. The blue background represents the Gulf of Mexico and Louisiana's many rivers and **wetlands.**

STATE NICKNAME: THE PELICAN STATE

In 1902 the Louisiana **legislature** chose "The Pelican State" as Louisiana's official nickname. It suggest that Louisiana, like the pelican, is dedicated to those in its care.

STATE SONGS

Louisiana adopted "Give Me Louisiana" as the state song in 1970. In 1977 lawmakers added a second state song— "You Are My Sunshine." It was written in 1931 and released in 1940 by Jimmie H. Davis, a musician who became Louisiana's governor in 1944. It is one of the most popular songs ever recorded.

"You Are My Sunshine"

The other night, dear
As I lay sleeping
I dreamed I held you in my arms.
When I awoke, dear
I was mistaken
And I hung my head and cried;
Chorus
You are my sunshine
My only sunshine
You make me happy
When skies are gray
You'll never know dear
How much I love you
Please don't take my sunshine away.

The magnolia blossom is about the size of a cup and saucer.

State Flower: Magnolia

Because they are a common sight across the state, the magnolia was named the state flower in 1900. The large, creamy white blossoms with their sweet scent represent the richness of Louisiana life.

A bald cypress can grow as high as 100 feet.

State Tree: Bald Cypress

The bald cypress thrives in Louisiana's bayous and **swamps.** It was named the official state tree in 1963. Louisiana lawmakers thought the long-lasting wood of the cypress reflected the strength of Louisianans. A bald cypress can even withstand the strong winds of a **hurricane.**

State Dog: Catahoula Leopard Dog

The Louisiana Catahoula Leopard Dog was chosen as the state dog in 1979. The breed can be traced to Native American Catahoula Lake hunting dogs and the dogs of Spanish explorers. These dogs have webbed feet that help them survive in Louisiana's swamps and **marshes.**

Hunters rely on Catahoula Leopard Dogs to track opossums, rabbits, and other animals.

State Bird: Brown Pelican

The eastern brown pelican became the state bird in 1966. Brown pelicans live along the Gulf coast. They use their large bills and pouches to scoop up fish.

State Crustacean: Crawfish

Lawmakers named the crawfish the state crustacean or shellfish in 1983. It looks like a small lobster with two front claws and a jointed shell. About 87 percent of the crawfish in the United States come from Louisiana.

A young pelican can eat six pounds of fish a day.

State Insect: Honeybee

Louisiana chose the honeybee as the state insect in 1977 for two reasons: honey is an important product in the state and the busy honeybee symbolizes the industry of hardworking Louisianans.

Crawfish are found in the shallow, muddy water of the bayous.

There are more than 1 million wild alligators in Louisiana. An additional 250,000 are raised on alligator farms.

STATE REPTILE: ALLIGATOR

Louisiana has the largest alligator population in the United States. Therefore lawmakers named the alligator the state reptile in 1983.

STATE GEMSTONE: AGATE

In 1976 the Louisiana legislature named the agate the state's official gemstone. Agate is a common stone found in gravel across the state.

When polished, the layered patterns inside an agate look like tiny landscapes.

Louisiana's History and People

The flags of Spain, France, Britain, and the United States have all flown over what is today Louisiana. Each nation has shaped life in the state, as have Native American groups.

NATIVE AMERICANS

When Europeans first came to Louisiana in the 1500s, Native Americans had been living there for nearly 12,000 years. By the early 1700s about 15,000 Native Americans from more than 20 different tribes lived in the area. Among them were the Caddo in the northwest along the Red River and the Natchez further south. In the late 1700s the Choctaw moved to Louisiana after being forced from their homes in the southeast by British settlers.

The Poverty Point Mounds

A people who lived near Monroe in northeastern Louisiana more than 3,500 years ago built earth mounds that stand 70 feet high. According to **archaeologists,** the builders used thousands of tons of earth to create the mounds over a period of more than 570 years. The mounds were probably used in religious ceremonies. Today, visitors can view the mounds from an observation tower at the Poverty Point Historic Site.

Spanish and French Heritage

In 1519 Alonso Alvarez de Piñeda, a Spanish explorer, spotted the Louisiana coast while exploring the Gulf of Mexico. About twenty years later Hernando de Soto sailed down the Mississippi River through Louisiana, almost to the river's mouth. The first explorer to reach the river's mouth was a French explorer René-Robert Cavelier, **Sieur de LaSalle.** In 1682 he claimed for France all of the land from the Mississippi River west to the Rocky Mountains, north to Canada, and south to the Gulf of Mexico.

In 1698 King Louis XIV sent the Le Moyne brothers, Bienville and Iberville, to protect France's claims to Louisiana. The next year Iberville founded a French **colony** in Louisiana. Even with the king's support, however, few French families wanted to settle in Louisiana. Many saw it as a wild **swamp** filled with insects and dangerous alligators. So the colony grew slowly. Still, in 1718 Bienville founded New Orleans on the site of a Native American village. Louisiana grew slowly in part because France was engaged in a costly war with Britain. As its expenses mounted, the government decided in a secret agreement in 1762 to turn the colony over to Spain.

Spanish Rule

Under Spanish rule, Louisiana's population grew. French Canadians settled near the bayous west of New Orleans and German settlers in the north-central part of the colony. Some newcomers came with slaves from West Africa and the Caribbean. Forced to work on the large **plantations** that sprang up in the **territory,** slaves grew the cotton, rice, and sugarcane that brought great wealth to Louisiana.

When the **American Revolutionary War** (1775–1783) began in 1775, Louisiana was home to about 50,000 people. After Spain declared war on Britain in 1779, Bernardo

Bienville is often called the "Father of Louisiana."

de Galvez, Louisiana's governor, opened the port of New Orleans to U.S. ships and sold supplies to the Americans. He also captured British forts along the lower Mississippi.

Louisiana Purchase, 1803

Not long after Britain's defeat in the American Revolutionary War, France took Louisiana back from Spain in an agreement signed in 1800. Three years later, France was once again in need of cash. This time it sold Louisiana to the United States. The sale is called the Louisiana Purchase.

At first, U.S. president Thomas Jefferson only wanted the port of New Orleans. He changed his mind when he realized the importance of controlling the entire Mississippi–Missouri river system. The purchase doubled the size of the United States at a cost of $15 million—just 4 cents an acre.

Statehood

In 1804 the U.S. government divided the Louisiana Purchase into three smaller territories—Louisiana, Missouri, and Orleans. On April 30, 1812, Orleans became the state of Louisiana.

The ceremony between the United States and France for the land transfer for the Louisiana Purchase took place in 1803.

THE CIVIL WAR IN LOUISIANA

Louisiana joined the **Confederacy** on January 26, 1861, shortly before the start of the **Civil War.** In April 1862 Union forces captured New Orleans. The Union army continued upriver and took Baton Rouge in early May. The Confederacy controlled much of inland Louisiana, however. The fighting destroyed many Louisiana farms and **plantations.** The state's economy would not improve much until the start of World War II in 1939.

FAMOUS PEOPLE

Zachary Taylor (1784–1850), U.S. president. Born in New Orleans, Taylor was a U.S. general who became the twelfth president of the United States in 1849.

Huey Pierce Long Jr. (1893–1935), politician. Born near Winfield, Long became governor in 1928. He improved education and transportation, built hospitals, and helped the poor. He also made enemies who questioned his methods. In 1932 Louisianans elected Long to the U.S. Senate. Three years later, a political enemy shot and killed him.

Huey Long often said he was on the side of the little man against big business.

Jose Ruiz De Rivera (1904–1985), sculptor. De Rivera was born in Baton Rouge. Many of his sculptures are steel or bronze bands twisted into three-dimensional shapes. They are on display in museums around the country.

Ernest J. Gaines (1933–), author. Gaines's books are based on his childhood on the River Lake plantation in Pointe Coupée Parish. He was the fifth generation in his family to be born there. Gaines is best known for *The Autobiography of Miss Jane Pittman,* the fictional story of an African American woman whose life spans a hundred years.

From 1997 to 2001, Lindy Boggs was the U.S. ambassador to the Vatican in Rome.

Corinne (Lindy) Claiborne Boggs (1916–), politician. Born in Pointe Coupee Parish, Boggs was elected to the U.S. House of Representatives in a special election in 1973 after her husband, Representative Wade Boggs, died in an airplane crash. The first woman from Louisiana to serve in Congress, she served nine terms.

While Ernest Morial was mayor of New Orleans, the city hosted the Louisiana World Exposition of 1984.

Ernest N. "Dutch" Morial (1929–1989), politican. Morial was the first African American to serve in the Louisiana legislature. He was also mayor of New Orleans from 1978 to 1986. He was the first African American to hold that office.

William Joyce (1957–), author and illustrator. Born in Shreveport, Joyce is known for such award-winning children's books as *Rolie Polie Olie, Dinosaur Bob,* and *George Shrinks.*

The French Quarter

The French Quarter is a district in the heart of New Orleans. The French Quarter is known for its historic buildings, tree-lined streets, vegetable and fruit markets, cafés, art galleries, and music.

A Planned City

In 1721 French engineer Adrien de Pauger laid out the original twenty blocks of New Orleans around the *Place d'Armes*, which means the "place of armies" in French. It is also called the *Vieux Carré*, which is French for "Old Square." After U.S. general Andrew Jackson defeated the British in the Battle of New Orleans during the War of 1812, the grateful citizens of New Orleans renamed the square in his honor in 1850. In 1856 they placed a statue of Jackson on a horse in the center of the square.

In 1848 the Baroness Pontalba, a wealthy Spanish developer, constructed apartment buildings a block long at each end of Jackson Square. These were the first apartment buildings in North America.

In 1921 the Pontalba family sold the Lower Pontalba building. It was given to the State Museum in 1927.

Mardi Gras

Every year, New Orleans throws a huge party in the French Quarter to celebrate Mardi Gras—

St. Louis Cathedral

Built in 1718, the St. Louis Cathedral is the oldest cathedral in the United States. Inside are stained glass windows. On the ceiling are paintings of angels and scenes from the Bible. The cathedral's white towers face Jackson Square.

the ten days before Lent. Lent is a period of 40 days during which Catholics fast by giving up certain foods.

The French Catholics brought Mardi Gras to Louisiana. The name means "Fat Tuesday," because the celebrations end on the Tuesday before Lent. New Orleans's first Mardi Gras parade was in 1838.

During Mardi Gras, members of various krewes, the organizations that sponsor the parades that mark the holiday, ride floats through the streets. They toss colorful beads and other prizes to the crowds that gather to watch. French settlers probably brought the custom to New Orleans. In the 1600s the French royal family and other nobles threw coins to the poor during Mardi Gras.

The word *krewe* is an old-fashioned way of spelling the word *crew*. Krewes work all year to prepare for Mardi Gras by raising money, building floats, and making costumes.

More than 500,000 people go to Mardi Gras, which has been called the "Greatest Free Show on Earth."

Louisiana's State Government

Baton Rouge has been the capital of Louisiana since 1882. Before then, the capital was moved several times. New Orleans, Donaldsonville, Opelousas, and Shreveport have all been the seat of state government at one time or another.

Louisiana's government is based on its constitution. A constitution explains how a government is supposed to work. Louisianans have had eleven different constitutions, more than any other U.S. state. Louisiana adopted its current constitution in 1975. Like the U.S. government, Louisiana's government is made up of three branches: the legislative, executive, and judicial.

Legislative Branch

The legislative branch makes Louisiana's laws. The state **legislature** is divided into two parts or houses—a senate and a house of representatives. Both meet each year for about two months. This is less than half the time most state legislatures meet.

The senate has 39 members and the house of representatives has 105. These men and women each represent

The 34-story capitol building in Baton Rouge is the tallest capitol in the United States.

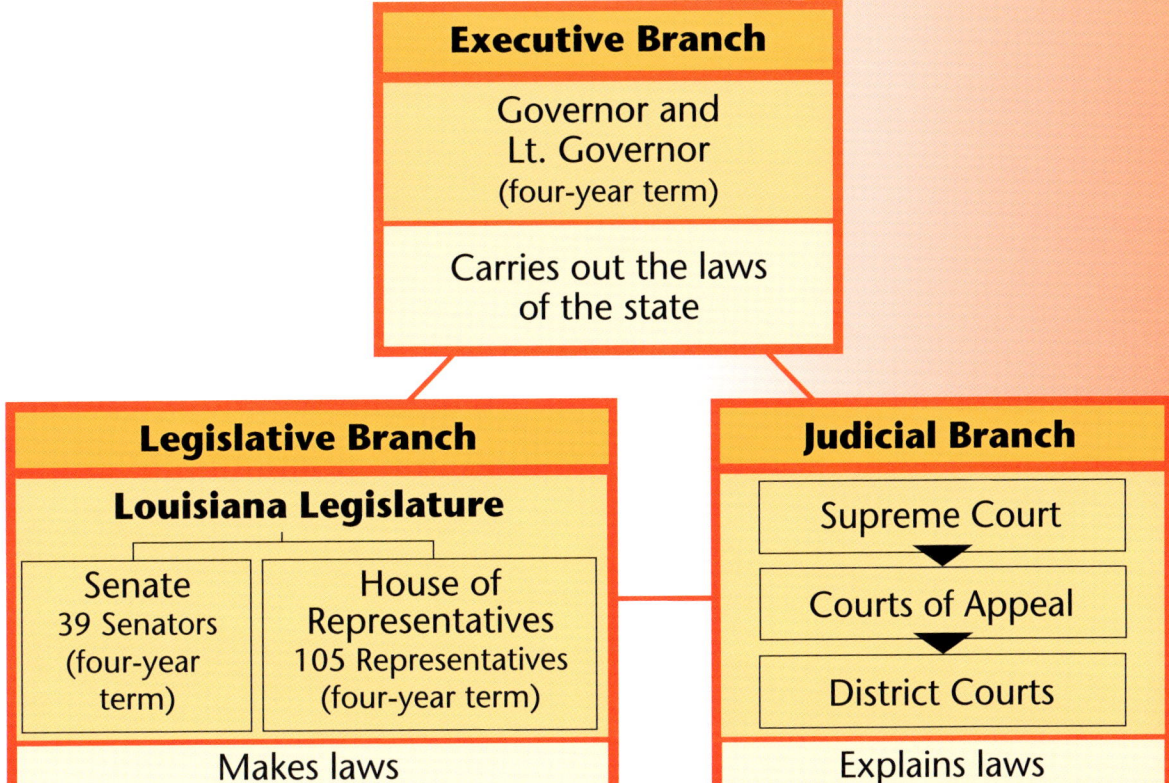

a district in the state. Both senators and representatives serve four-year terms.

The house of representatives proposes, researches, and writes laws. The senate holds meetings to debate and rework bills, as proposed laws are known. When majorities in both houses agree on a bill, it is sent to the governor for approval. If the governor signs the bill, it becomes law. If the governor rejects the bill, or vetoes it, the bill is sent back to the legislature. The legislature can overturn a veto if a two-thirds majority in each house votes to do so.

Louisiana's Parishes

Louisiana is divided into parishes. A parish is what a county is called in Louisiana. The word reflects the influence of the French and Spanish on the state. Both are Catholics. The Catholic Church uses the word *parish* for a township or cluster of townships with its own church and priest. There are 64 parishes in the state. Most parishes have elected councils that are responsible for such things as road repair and police protection.

Executive Branch

The executive branch is responsible for enforcing state laws. The head of Louisiana's executive branch is the governor, who serves a four-year term. The governor also prepares the state budget and manages the day-to-day operations of the state. The lieutenant governor steps in if the governor is unable to carry out his or her job. The lieutenant governor also serves as commissioner of the Department of Culture, Recreation, and Tourism. Other elected state officials include a **secretary of state, attorney general,** and **treasurer.**

Judicial Branch

The judicial branch of government decides how the state's laws apply to particular cases. Louisiana has 5 courts of appeal and 40 district courts that handle a wide variety of cases. The Louisiana Supreme Court has a chief justice and six associate justices. They are all elected for ten-year terms. The justices make decisions about cases that have come to them from lower courts. All Louisiana judges are elected.

Civil Law

Louisiana's legal system is different from that of other states. It is based on the **Napoleonic code** of France. In Louisiana judges use a strict set of rules to make decisions in legal cases. In other states, judges rely on **precedent** in making decisions. That means they decide cases based on what judges have ruled in similar cases.

The Louisiana Supreme Court is the highest court in the state.

Louisiana's Culture

Louisianans use the French phrase *joie de vivre,* which means "the joy of living," to describe their unique approach to life. This joy is seen in their many cultural events and in their music.

A Diverse Heritage

Louisiana is home to Native Americans, Europeans, Africans, Caribbean islanders, **Cajuns,** and other groups. Each has added its own special flavor to the state.

Louisiana's music reflects its cultural diversity. Each group that settled in the state has contributed to the sounds associated with Louisiana, whether it is in African American folk songs, Cajun bands at local fairs, country dances held in southern Louisiana, the community hymn singings of northern Louisiana, or the jazz sounds of New Orleans.

Jazz

The beginnings of jazz can be traced back to slaves who were taken from West Africa to the Caribbean and then to Louisiana **plantations.**

In 2001 New Orleans named its airport after Louis Armstrong.

There, the unique African and Caribbean sounds and beats blended with the music of European settlers. A hint of European brass bands can be heard in jazz's horn and drum sounds. Jazz bands usually have a trumpet, a drum, a bass, and a piano.

Louis Armstrong (1900–1971) was born in New Orleans. He sang and danced for pennies in the streets of the French Quarter when he was five years old. When he grew up, he became known as a musician, singer, and bandleader. He is considered one of the founders of jazz. The music he played on his trumpet can be heard today on television and radio and in movies. He also had his own unique singing style. He used his gravelly voice to imitate various instruments.

A New Orleans tradition is the jazz funeral. A jazz band slowly marches the grieving family to the cemetery playing sad songs. When the family is ready to leave the cemetery, the band starts playing happy tunes, dancing back down the street.

Cajun and Zydeco Music

In 1755 several thousand French-speaking people fled Acadia in eastern Canada. Forced from their homes by the British, they came to Louisiana in hopes that they

The New Orleans jazz funeral comes from African burial traditions that are hundreds of years old.

A frottoir is a washboard instrument and gives a raspy background sound to Cajun music.

would be able to practice their Catholic faith and keep their language alive. Many settled along the Mississippi River near Bayou Teche and Bayou Lafourche. Some intermarried with the Chitimacha people. Over the years, the Acadians became known as Cajuns. Listeners can still hear the rich and sad sounds of ancient French songs in their music.

The New Orleans Jazz and Heritage Festival

Every year during the last week in April and the first week in May, thousands of music lovers from all over the world flock to Louisiana for the New Orleans Jazz and Heritage Festival. More than 4,000 musicians, cooks, and artists host the 400,000 or more people who come to the festival every year. The ten-day event features concerts performed by the best jazz, rhythm and blues, gospel, and **zydeco** musicians in the world. Recent performers include Bob Dylan, Fats Domino, and Crosby, Stills and Nash.

An iron triangle and a fiddle, or violin, are central to the Cajun sound. A washboard provides the background rhythm. Louisiana's official musical instrument, the accordion, was added later to the unique Cajun sound. A near relation of Cajun music is zydeco. Zydeco has the Cajun sound and uses some of the same instruments, but guitars and a faster beat give it a rock-country sound.

Gospel Music

Gospel music can be heard in churches across Louisiana. Drums, tambourines, piano, and organ accompany great harmonies and lively, soulful singing. The music blends African rhythms with Christian themes. Mahalia Jackson (1911–1972) was of many gospel singers whose singing began in church choirs in and around New Orleans.

"Making a joyful noise" is what gospel choirs in Louisiana are all about.

Louisiana's Food

Served with Louisiana's unique history is a healthy helping of spicy and rich foods. The mix of Native American, African, West Indian, European, and Cajun food is typical in Louisiana. The state's restaurants feature fresh shrimp, oysters, crab, crawfish, and fish in dishes like jambalaya, spicy rice with seafood or meat, and gumbo.

CREOLE CUISINE

Creole food combines the best of French, Spanish, and African American recipes. Gumbo, a Cajun–Creole stew that is a mix of seafood, vegetables, meats, and spices, is an example of this combination of cultures. Red beans and rice, a Spanish dish, is also a popular dish.

French and Spanish Creole restaurants offer fresh baked breads, crawfish bisque, Oysters Bienville, and other European-style dishes served with a Louisiana flair. Crawfish bisque is a thick soup made with crawfish, rice, onions, and other vegetables. It is spiced with a crawfish boil seasoning that has ground hot red peppers as its main ingredient. Oysters Bienville, named for the founder of New Orleans, is served on oyster shells and covered by a creamy white sauce with shrimp and mushrooms and topped with bread crumbs and grated cheese. To really experience Creole cooking, visitors have to taste a *beignet,* a lighter-than-air French pastry that is covered with powdered sugar.

Gumbo

The word *gumbo* comes from an African word for okra, a green vegetable widely grown in the South. **Ask an adult to help you with this recipe.**

- 3 tablespoons vegetable oil
- 3 tablespoons flour
- 1 large chopped onion
- 1 cup chopped celery
- 1 cup chopped green pepper
- 1 can tomato sauce
- 1 pound okra cooked and sliced
- 5 to 6 cloves
- 1 can tomatoes
- 2 to 3 cups water
- 1 teaspoon of sugar
- salt and pepper to taste
- 1 bay leaf
- 1 tablespoon chopped parsley or cilantro
- 2 pounds shelled and deveined shrimp

Heat the vegetable oil in a skillet. Stir in flour and keep stirring until flour is browned. Then add onion, celery, cloves, and green pepper. Stir in tomato sauce and mix thoroughly. In another saucepan, fry the okra until it is slightly browned. Add the okra and a can of tomatoes to the first mixture. Cook slowly, adding water a little bit at a time. Add sugar, salt, and pepper.

Let the dish cook over a low heat, simmering for about an hour. Add the bay leaf and shrimp and cook for a half an hour. Serve over steamed rice. Top with parsley or cilantro.

CREOLE AND CAJUN FOOD IN THE FRENCH QUARTER

Antoine's is one of the oldest family-owned restaurants in the United States. It was established in 1840 by Antoine Alciatore, a French immigrant. Its serves European and Creole dishes. The restaurant has served more than 3 million orders of Oysters Rockefeller, its famous shellfish and spinach dish, since it was first placed on the menu in 1899.

Other restaurants in the French Quarter serve pompano en papillote. The recipe calls for fish baked in a paper bag until tender and flaky and then served in a wine sauce.

Po-boy sandwiches earned the name "poor-boy" because they are inexpensive and contain all the ingredients found in a full-course meal.

LOUISIANA PO-BOY

Some of Louisiana's best dishes are not served at Antoine's or other fancy restaurants. One of the most famous is a stuffed sandwich made with french bread. It is called a poor boy, or po-boy. Po-boys can be stuffed with almost anything—fried shrimp, oysters, catfish, roast beef, chicken, meatballs, deli meats, and even french fries. However, they are always served on slices of french or sourdough bread.

Louisiana's Folklore and Legends

The word *folklore* means stories, music, games, and other things that are passed from generation to generation. Folktales can teach us lessons or help us remember a person or event. Legends are true stories that have been exaggerated over the years. It sometimes is hard to know what is true and what is not.

JEAN LAFITTE'S GHOST SHIP

During the War of 1812, the British asked a French pirate for his help in attacking New Orleans. The pirate Jean Lafitte (1780–1825) operated out of the port of New Orleans. Instead of aiding the British, Lafitte sided with the Americans. Lafitte's raids of British ships helped the Americans win the Battle of New Orleans on January 8, 1815. After the war, Lafitte returned to his pirate ways. He disappeared in 1825.

Before he was a pirate, Lafitte was a blacksmith in New Orleans.

What happened to him and his pirate treasure remains a mystery.

According to one legend, when the moon is full, Lafitte and his crew sail to Grand Island off the coast of Louisiana looking for the gold and jewels they buried long ago. Many people still come to Grand Island to search for treasure. They return home with tales of ghostly pirate ships but without riches.

MOSQUITO, LAPIN, AND LOUP GAROU

African American, Creole, and **Cajun** folk stories are told and retold in Louisiana. Two popular stories involve Lapin, a wily rabbit, and Loup Garou, a shadowy figure who sometimes takes the form of a wolf.

In one of the most famous Lapin stories, Rat and Possum decide to punish the rabbit Lapin for stealing their well water. They place a figure made of tar by a well and wait. When Lapin sees the doll, he thinks it is real and attacks it. When Possum and Rat arrive, they find him stuck fast to the doll.

Many of the characters in the Uncle Remus stories are based on Louisiana folktales.

Another favorite Cajun story features Loup Garou. He likes to help hard-working fishers. Many stories tell of oystermen who after a day at sea fall into an exhausted sleep. When they awake the next morning, their oysters are mysteriously cleaned. One night a curious fisher decides to find out who cleaned his oysters. When he sees a shadowy form with a long tail cleaning the shellfish one at a time, he cries out. The noise frightens Loup Garou. He disappears into thin air and never returns again.

Louisiana's Sports Teams

Sports fans in Louisiana root for many exciting professional and college teams. Louisianans are known for strongly supporting their teams year after year.

PROFESSIONAL SPORTS

The National Football League's New Orleans Saints football team got its start in 1966. The Saints 1967–1968 season of seven wins, twenty losses, and one tie was the best ever two-year record for an expansion club. In 2000 the Saints had a standout year when they tied for the division championship. Although the Saints have often struggled, the fans are more excited about their team

The Louisiana Superdome

The Louisiana Superdome soars high above the New Orleans skyline. The top of the dome is 30 stories high and seats more than 69,000 people. It is the largest covered stadium in the world.

than ever. The Saints play in the Superdome, one of the world's largest arenas.

The Superdome has hosted six Super Bowl championship games and four National Collegiate Athletic Association men's basketball championships. Each year, in early January, the Superdome hosts the Sugar Bowl, one of the best-known collegiate championship games in college football. Tulane University football games also are played at the Superdome.

The National Basketball Association team, the Hornets, came to New Orleans in 2002. The team adopted Mardi Gras colors—purple, gold, white, and teal—for its team logo. In 2003 a crowd of 18,509, the largest in New Orleans Arena history, watched as the Los Angeles Lakers, led by former Louisiana State University (LSU) star Shaquille O'Neal, defeated the Hornets.

The Hornets hold the eighth-best winning percentage in the NBA over the last six years.

LSU's Tiger Stadium holds more than 90,000 people and is the fourth largest on-campus college football stadium in the country.

College Sports

LSU in Baton Rouge is home to the LSU Tigers. In the fall of 1896, coach A.W. Jeardeau's LSU football team posted a perfect 6-0 record. After that football season, LSU adopted the nickname. It comes from a volunteer company in the **Confederate** Army nicknamed the Tiger Rifles. The volunteers organized in New Orleans in 1861, the year the **Civil War** began. In 1936 LSU students purchased a Bengal tiger as a mascot for the team.

The most famous moment in LSU Tiger Stadium's history took place on October 8, 1988. That night, LSU's Tommy Hodson threw the ball to Eddie Fuller for a winning touchdown against Auburn University. The roar of the crowd was so loud that it caused an earth tremor. The tremor was recorded on a special meter in LSU's geology department across campus.

Louisiana's Businesses and Products

Louisiana's location on the Gulf of Mexico and the Mississippi River Delta gives the state some unique advantages. It is rich in natural resources and its ports have access to the markets around the world.

Farming and Logging

With its mild climate, Louisiana is a leader in a wide range of farm products. It is second in the United States in the production of sugarcane, sweet potatoes, and soybeans, third in rice production, fifth in pecans, and sixth in cotton.

With more than 13 million acres of pine, gum, oak, and cypress trees, the lumber industry is booming in Louisiana. One-half of all matches produced in the United States are made there. The matches are a combination of wood and sulphur—two products readily available in the state.

Oil

In 1901 Louisiana's first oil well was drilled in Jennings on Jules Clément's farm. More than

Offshore oil-well platforms allow workers to bring up oil and gas from underneath the seabed.

100 years later, that well is still producing oil. Today Louisiana is the third largest refiner of oil products in the United States. Much of the oil and natural gas come from the Gulf of Mexico. The world's largest fleet of private helicopters is located in Morgan City. The helicopters carry oil workers to and from offshore oil wells in the Gulf of Mexico.

Fishing

Louisiana produces about 25 percent of all the seafood in the United States, including tuna, catfish, shrimp, oysters, crawfish, and crabs. Louisiana's most famous product is crawfish, a popular food in the South and Southwest. It is also considered a delicacy in Central America and in European countries such as Spain, France, and Portugal. In Louisiana more than 1,600 farmers produce crawfish in ponds, and more than 800 commercial fishers harvest crawfish from natural **wetlands.**

Fishers harvest shrimp and oysters in the Gulf of Mexico.

Tourism

Louisiana is known as the "Sportsman's Paradise." Each year many thousands of people apply for permits to hunt and fish in Louisiana. Other tourists take advantage of Louisiana's opportunities for hiking or bird-watching in wetland areas. Mardi Gras

The Alligator Industry

Native Americans and early settlers used alligator skins for coats and boots. By the 1930s people were using the skins to make purses, belts, and shoes. Many, especially Cajuns in southern Louisiana, also ate the meat of the alligator. In the early 1960s the state outlawed alligator hunting. The number of alligators was dropping, as a result of too much harvesting. By 1971 the alligator population began to rise and hunting was allowed again. Louisiana began an alligator ranching program in 1986. Farmers are required to return fourteen percent of their healthy, four-foot or larger alligators to the wild each year. The rest can be sold for food or skins.

and the sights of New Orleans, beautiful historic **plantation** homes around the state, and music festivals draw tourists from around the world. Tourism brings in $8.7 billion to Louisiana each year, making it one of the state's most important industries.

A canopy of giant oak trees, planted before the house was built, stretches more than a quarter mile in front of Oak Alley Plantation in Vacherie.

Attractions and Landmarks

Louisiana brings to mind old **plantation** houses, crawfish festivals, and Mardi Gras. However, there are many other things to see and do in the Pelican State. The attractions are discussed starting from the northern part of the state and heading south.

NORTH AND CENTRAL LOUISIANA

Marie Thérese Coincoin, a freed slave, founded Melrose Plantation in 1786 near Natchitoches. On the 68 acres of land she received from her former master, she built a plantation that earned enough money to buy the free-

Clementine Hunter

Clementine Hunter (1886–1988), a self-taught folk artist, was born on a cotton plantation near Cloutierville, Louisiana. In the late 1920s Hunter began working as a cook at Melrose Plantation. She started painting when she was in her 40s, creating scenes of everyday life. She also painted pictures of plants and animals common to Louisiana. Hunter was the first African American artist to have a show at the New Orleans Museum of Art. She is considered one of Louisiana's most famous artists.

Places to See in Louisiana

dom of her enslaved children. The plantation developed into one of the largest communities of free blacks in northern Louisiana.

The Audubon State Commemorative Area includes the old English town of St. Francisville and the Oakley Plantation House. There, the illustrator James Audubon began or completed 32 of his famous Birds of America series in 1821. Birds of America is a series of more than 400 paintings of different types of North American birds.

Southern Louisiana

The Longfellow–Evangeline State Historic Area is a 157-acre park 30 minutes southeast of Lafayette. Visitors can see several Acadian houses from the 1700s and visit a museum that tells of the Acadians' journey from Nova Scotia in the mid-1700s.

Near the Bayou Teche in St. Martinville stands the Evangeline Oak. This huge oak tree was made famous by Henry Wadsworth Longfellow in his poem *Evangeline: A Tale of Acadia.* The poem is based on a true story. It tells of the young Acadian girl Evangeline who waits by the oak for the boy she is engaged to. He never keeps their meeting.

The Delta Queen Steamboat Company offers tours along the Mississippi River, from New Orleans to Baton Rouge, Natchez, and other riverside cities. River tours

As in the 1800s, the famous Delta Queen *steamboat runs from Pittsburgh all the way south to New Orleans.*

The aquarium complex has an underwater oil rig that shows how coral and other marine animals transform such structures into a habitat.

on the *Delta Queen* last from three to twelve days. Stops are made at historic sites such as plantations and old settlements.

Another old boat, the *Natchez,* is anchored in New Orleans. Visitors can take a two-hour tour of the Mississippi on the *Natchez* and tour the different parts of the steamboat. The *Natchez* has a 32-note calliope, a keyboard instrument that looks a little like a church organ. The boat's paddlewheel is made of 25 tons of white oak. The paddlewheel propels the steamboat down the river.

The Audubon Aquarium of the Americas is located on the banks of the Mississippi River in New Orleans. With four major underwater habitats or living environments—a Caribbean reef, an oil rig, a Mississippi delta, and the Gulf—the aquarium is home to more than 7,500 marine creatures.

Built in 1835, the Old U.S. Mint in New Orleans turned out coins for the United States until 1909. It was a federal prison in the 1930s and then used by the Coast Guard as a southeastern headquarters until the 1970s. Since the late 1970s, the state has used the building as a museum dedicated to the history of jazz in New

The exhibits at the D-Day Museum take visitors through the weeks and days leading up to D-Day, which occurred on June 6, 1944.

Orleans. The story of jazz is told through instruments, paintings, recordings, and photographs.

The National D-Day Museum, which opened in 2000, is the only museum in the United States that showcases all of the land-to-sea invasions or "d-days" of **World War II.** It is located in New Orleans because it was there that Andrew Higgins built the boats used in the land-to-sea invasions during the war. President Eisenhower once said that Higgins's boats won the war for the Allies.

SWAMP GARDENS

Located near Morgan City, Swamp Gardens is a living museum in a three-acre swamp. Ducks, turtles, squirrels, and deer roam freely, while alligators, otters, owls, and snapping turtles may be observed within cages. Cabins and lifelike figures throughout the park show what life was like for people who used to live in the area, including Native Americans, fishers, and trappers.

Map of Louisiana

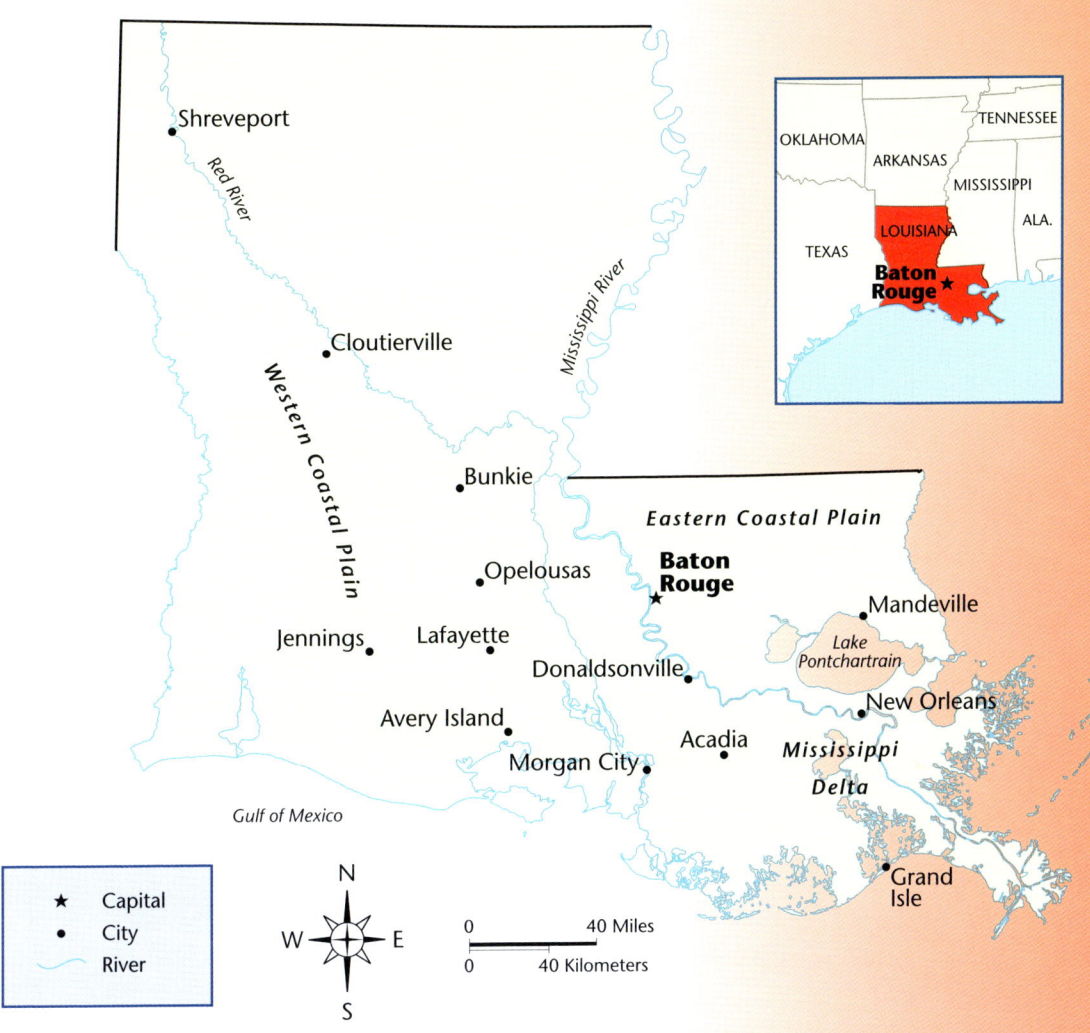

Glossary

American Revolutionary War (1775–1783) the war for American independence between the colonists and Great Britain

archaeologists scientists who study the physical remains of past cultures

attorney general chief law officer of a state

Cajun a person related to the Acadians who came to Louisiana in the mid-1700s from present-day eastern Canada

causeway a raised roadway across a body of water

Civil War (1861–1865) the war in the United States between the northern states loyal to the Union and the southern states loyal to the Confederacy

colony a settlement in a distant land that is under the authority of the settler's homeland

Confederacy the eleven southern states that left the United States in 1861 and formed their own government

Creole a person whose family originally came to Louisiana from France, Spain, and Africa.

culture customs and beliefs shared by a people

delta soil and material deposited over long periods of time by a river at its mouth

legislature an elected body of officials who make laws for a state or nation

levee a dirt or concrete wall built to keep rivers and seas from flooding

heritage the history and culture of a family, community, or nation

hurricane an ocean-born storm with continuing winds of at least 74 miles per hour

marsh a wetland where no trees grow

Napoleonic Code created by Napolean, a French emperor, in 1804, a code of law that contains civil laws but not criminal laws

oil refining when oil is made into gasoline and other products

plantation a large farm where cash crops are raised

precedent an act that can be used as an example for future acts

secretary of state public official responsible for keeping state records

Sieur de Iberville Sir of Iberville, a French royal title

Sieur de LaSalle Sir of LaSalle, a French royal title

swamp a wetland where trees grow

territory an area of land and water under the rule of a nation, state

treasurer person in charge of the money of a government

wetlands a low area of land that is covered with water

World War II (1941–1945) international conflict between the United States and its allies versus Germany, Japan, and Italy

zydeco popular music of southern Louisiana that combines elements of French and Caribbean music and the blues, played on the guitar, the accordion, and a washboard

More Books to Read

Doucet, Sharon. *Lapin Plays Possum: Trickster Tales from the Louisiana Bayou.* New York: Farrar, Straus and Giroux, 2002.

Fonténot, Nicole Denee. *Cooking with Cajun Women, Recipes and Remembrances from South Louisiana.* New York: Hippocrene Press, 2002.

Grimm, Phyllis W. *Crayfish.* Minneapolis, Minn.: Lerner Publications, 2001.

Hintz, Martin. *Louisiana.* New York: Children's Press, 1998.

Jaffe, Elizabeth D. *The Louisiana Purchase.* Mankato, Minn.: Bridgestone Books, 2002.

Index

accordion, 28
agate, 14
alligators, 9, 13, 39
American Revolutionary War, 16
archeologists, 15
Armstrong, Luis, 26
attorney general, 24
Audubon Aquarium of the Americas, 43
Audubon State Commemorative Area, 41
Avery Island, 8–9

bald cypress, 12
Baton Rouge, 4–5, 17
Battle of New Orleans, 20, 32
bayou, 7, 12
Boggs, Corinne "Lindy" Claiborne, 19
brown pelican, 12

Cajun, 25, 27, 33
Cajun and zydeco music, 26–28
Catahoula Leopard Dog, 12
Civil War, 17, 36
Claiborne, William C.C., 10
climate, 7
Coincoin, Marie Thérèse, 40
colony, 16
Confederacy, 17, 36
crawfish, 13
culture, 25–28

De Rivera, Jose Ruiz, 18
delta, 6
Delta Queen, 42

Eastern Coastal Plain, 6
Evangeline Oak, 42

farming, 37
fishing, 38
folklore, 32–33
food, 29–31
French Opera House, 8
French Quarter, 20–21, 31

Gaines, Ernest J., 18
gospel music, 28

government
 civil law, 24
 executive branch, 24
 judicial branch, 24
 legislative branch, 22–23
gumbo (recipe), 30

honeybee, 14
Hunter, Clementine, 40
hurricane, 12

Iberville, Sieur de, 4

Jackson, Mahalia, 28
jazz, 25–26
Jefferson, Thomas, 17
Joyce, William, 19

krewes, 21

Lafitte, Jean, 32–33
Lake Ponchartrain, 6
Lake Ponchartrain Causeway, 9
LaSalle, Sieur de, 4, 16
legislature, 11, 22–23
levee, 5
logging, 37
Long, Huey Pierce, Jr., 18
Longfellow–Evangeline State Historic Area, 42–43
Louisiana Purchase, 17
Louisiana Superdome, 34
LSU Tigers, 36

magnolia, 12
Mahalia Jackson Theater, 8
Mardi Gras, 20–21
marsh, 6, 12
Melrose Plantation, 40
Morial, Ernest N., 19

Napoleonic code, 24
National D–Day Museum, 44
Native Americans, 15
New Orleans, 5, 16, 17
New Orleans Jazz and Heritage Festival, 27
New Orleans Saints, 34

oil, 37–38
Old U.S. Mint, 43–44

parishes, 24
plantations, 16, 17, 39, 40
po-boy, 31
Poverty Point mounds, 15
precedent, 24

secretary of state, 24
Shreveport, 5
slavery, 16
sports, 34–36
St. Louis Cathedral, 21
state symbols
 bird, 12
 crustacean, 13
 dog, 12
 flag, 11
 flower, 12
 gemstone, 14
 insect, 14
 motto, 10
 nickname, 11
 reptile, 13
 seal, 10
 song, 11
 tree, 12
statehood, 17
swamp, 7, 12
Swamp Gardens, 44

Tabasco sauce, 9
Tally-Ho Club, 8
Taylor, Zachary, 18
territory, 16
tourism, 38–39
treasurer, 24

War of 1812, 32
Western Coastal Plain, 6–7
wetlands, 7, 11, 38
World War II, 44

"You Are My Sunshine" (song), 11

About the Authors

Donna Loughran is an author and artist who lives in Austin, Texas. Since childhood, journeys into Louisiana and its backroads have been a fact of life. She has published many nonfiction books and interactive educational products for young readers and adults.

Chris Olson is a writer and editor who lives in Atlanta, Georgia. She has also lived in Texas and Missouri and traveled through much of Louisiana. She enjoys hiking and camping across the United States.